Then &

MARPLE AND

The scene looking up Stockport Road from Possett Bridge in the early 1900s. The bridge over the canal, built in 1804, has three openings, a horse tunnel, the main canal route and a blocked up entrance to the, now filled in, arm that used to go to the lime kiln complex. It is said that Samuel Oldknow offered possets of ale to the workmen to encourage them to quickly complete the canal at that point.

The view down the Stockport Road has not changed greatly in a hundred years. Children do not gather to watch a photographer today. The men sitting with their backs to the road on the lock gates are not interested at all. Today, unless the time was chosen very carefully, no one would stand in the middle of the road! In recent years a footpath was constructed alongside the bridge so that pedestrians would not be mown down in the traffic. The Liberal Club on the right hand side of the picture is no longer there; demolished in the 1980s its place has been taken by houses.

Then & Now
MARPLE AND MELLOR

COMPILED BY ANN HEARLE AND PETER CLARKE

TEMPUS

In the foreground is the railway viaduct, behind is the aqueduct that carries the Peak Forest Canal. They cross the steep valley of the River Goyt. They are a magnificent sight viewed from all angles. The canal aqueduct, 309 feet long and 100 feet above the river, took seven years to build and was opened in 1800. A severe frost in 1962 damaged the lining, allowing water to leak out and causing a collapse of the masonry on one side. It was feared that the aqueduct would not be repaired, but a vigorous campaign led to its restoration. The railway viaduct, with twelve stone arches and 124 feet above the river, only took one year to build, April 1862 to April 1863, despite being a much larger structure.

First published 2002

Tempus Publishing Limited
The Mill, Brimscombe Port,
Stroud, Gloucestershire, GL5 2QG

British Library Cataloguing in Publication Data.
A catalogue record for this book is available from the British Library.

ISBN 0 7524 2644 3

Typesetting and origination by Tempus Publishing Limited
Printed in Great Britain by Midway Colour Print, Wiltshire

CONTENTS

An empty Stockport Road. Many of the buildings in the picture were demolished in the last century. The 'Place', the old cottage on the right, went in the slum clearances of the 1930s. It was the birthplace of Judge John Bradshaw, the brother of the Henry Bradshaw who built Marple Hall. His was the first name on the execution warrant of Charles I. Its place has been taken by the Texaco garage. Behind the house was a smithy; the site is now a small green area with trees.

At the far end of the road can be seen Hollins Mill, which was demolished in the 1950s. On the left-hand side the wall and cottages were also raised to the ground. The site remained empty for many years until, eventually, a small parade of shops was built. The buildings stretching into the distance still remain, a mixture of shops, houses, a garage, doctor's surgery and a restaurant.

ACKNOWLEDGEMENTS

Ann and Peter would like to thank the many people who have helped them in any way, especially those who willingly lent us their old photographs and recounted their memories of people and events. In particular David Brindley, who from far off Anglesey gave advice on the technique of taking black and white photographs, and developed and printed the 'now' pictures. We do hope we have not missed anyone out, please excuse us if we have forgotten anybody: Marple Local History Society, Mark Whitaker, Charles Battersby, Denis Davies, Miss Broome, Jack Frogatt, Kath Rowson, Derek and Christine Newton, Mr and Mrs Bradley, Lesley Exley, Pat Booth, Walter Thorpe, Heather Brough, Marshall and Sheila Shaw, Mark Shaw, Mark Singleton, Ray Noble, Graeme Brock, Cedrick Beetham, Anthony Ashton, Jack Turnbull, Paul and Margaret Biddulph, Peacefield School, All Saints School, Ludworth School. Also three photographs by kind permission of Stockport Heritage Library.

INTRODUCTION

The district of Marple is situated at the south-eastern corner of the Manchester conurbation, with the hills of the Pennines as a back drop. It includes the 'villages' of Marple, Hawk Green, High Lane, Marple Bridge, Mellor, Strines and the hamlet of Mill Brow. The district is just over 11 square miles and includes much attractive countryside as well as the built up areas. It rises from 300ft by the River Goyt to just over 1,000ft on Cobden Edge. On a clear day it is possible to view the counties of Cheshire, Derbyshire, Lancashire, Yorkshire and some parts of Wales. The population grew from almost 13,000 just after the last war to approximately 27,000 in the early 1990s. Over two thirds of its 7,000 acres are included in the Greater Manchester Green Belt. The Macclesfield Canal meets the Peak Forest Canal in Marple, the latter's flight of 16 locks being the second steepest in the country. With its 300ft wide aqueduct, it is one of the main attractions and defines the character of the district.

The area around Mellor Church has been inhabited for over ten thousand years. Beginning with Mesolithic hunter gatherers, there then followed the Brigantes with their Iron Age Hill Fort, the Romans with a possible signal station, and the generations of Saxon, Mediaeval and modern day inhabitants.

From before the time of the Normans the district comprised small farms and hamlets, where the people made a living from the land and supplemented their incomes with the production of textiles in their homes. The minor gentry lived in the Halls in Marple and Mellor.

In the last quarter of the eighteenth century, one large and several smaller cotton spinning mills were erected in Mellor. Samuel Oldknow constructed the biggest, powered by the River Goyt. He changed the face of the whole area with the building of his mill, roads, the Peak Forest Canal, lime kilns, coal mines, workers housing and rebuilt farms. It was not until the 1830s that the Hollins Mill was erected in the area that became the centre of Marple. The families - the Carvers and the Hodgkinsons - who took over the enterprise in the late 1850s had a tremendous impact on the growth of the village and influenced every activity whether social, religious, educational, political or recreational for over fifty years. In the middle of the 1850s over half the working population, which included many young children, earned their living in the textile trades and a quarter in mines, quarries and farms.

The mills in Mellor had all disappeared by the end of the nineteenth century and Marple's Hollins Mill closed in the 1950s. The coalmines no longer exist. With the coming of the railway in 1862, villas, large and small for the new commuters, businessmen and their clerks, began to be built. The major growth of the area was after the end of the Second World War, and the constraints of the new Green Belt saved the area from further expansion. There was the loss of many old houses and cottages, including the demolition of the Jacobean Marple Hall. If only these buildings had survived a few more years they would surely have been saved.

The counties were established in Saxon times with the river Goyt the boundary between Cheshire and Derbyshire. In 1936 the old townships of Mellor and Ludworth were 'moved' from Derbyshire to Cheshire and became part of Marple Urban District! In 1974 the MUDC was abolished and the area became part of Stockport Metropolitan Borough in the County of Greater Manchester. The County still remains but the Greater Manchester Council was abolished in yet another change in recent years. Now except for the school and the Women's Institute, Ludworth is an almost forgotten name because the post office calls much of it, and also parts of Mellor and Lower Marple, Marple Bridge.

One of the authors is Ann Hearle, chairman of Marple Local History Society, who has lived in Mellor for over thirty years. First curious about the industrial history of the area, she is now interested in all of its past. This includes the times of the Romans and even further back, since the recent exciting discoveries around Mellor Church. She has collected photographs and old postcards of Marple and Mellor for many years.

The other author is Peter Clarke who has lived in Marple since 1979. His interest in the history of the area grew during his twenty years as a fireman based at Marple Fire Station. With a particular fascination in the events and people from the period around the First World War, he has co-researched the lives and deaths of those men from Marple remembered on Marple's War Memorials.

The Georgian church (Samuel Oldknow's church) had by 1964 become derelict. It was in a dangerous condition and was uninsurable. It was demolished leaving the tower and four foot high walls of the chancel and nave. The tower was strengthened and the bells were re-hung. Thus Marple has a free standing Bell Tower. In a corner of the tower is the memorial stone to Samuel Oldknow. It originally stood in the nave. Amongst the long inscription about his life and works are the words, 'Nor let this monument fail to record that to his unwearied exertions and generous munificence the inhabitants of this chapelry are chiefly indebted for the erection of this sacred edifice. A blessing which he rendered still more valuable by the influence of his example in constantly attending both the morning and evening services of Divine worship on every Sabbath day'. The photograph shows the arrival of the bells prior to the re-hanging.

Of all the buildings that Marple has lost, the Jacobean Hall was by far the greatest. The original farmhouse on the site was almost entirely rebuilt by Henry Bradshaw in 1659. A few years later new barns and stables were added by his son. More alterations were made in the early 1800s. After 1920 the hall was often left empty and the contents were eventually sold by auction in 1929. The loss of the caretaker led to increasing vandalism until in 1959 the Hall, because of its dangerous condition, was demolished by Marple Council. The photograph was taken in the early 1950s.

In 1960 Marple Hall Grammar School for boys was built and opened, followed by a school for girls in 1965. In 1974 the two schools combined and became comprehensive. Now, in 2002, it is used for eleven to sixteen year olds. The buildings are very much of the sixties!

Chapter 1
MARPLE AND
HAWK GREEN

The old photograph is from the early 1900s. The Hare and Hounds on Dooley Lane was built during the last quarter of the 18th century. The main road followed a route alongside what is today the pub car park, negotiating a very sharp narrow bend between the corner of the pub and the river bank. With the increase in motor traffic in the last century there was an equivalent increase in the number of serious accidents.

There was a row of cottages next to the Hare and Hounds on what is now the car park. Eleven of them were pulled down in the late 1950s and two others attached to the pub on the Marple side came down later. With the removal of the cottages the road was re-routed to the other side of the building, thus removing the dangerous bend.

The pub has been extensively modernised in recent years and an attractive beer garden added. Some trade must come from the many visitors to the nearby enormous garden centre.

The gates to Marple Hall were impressive. The photo was taken before the ribbon development of Stockport Road in the 1930s and the building of the Marple Hall estate in the 1960s. Until the start of the twentieth century, apart from the Rose Hill Cottages, there were no houses along the road, until the junction with Station Road. At that time the estate covered 520 acres. The Isherwoods started to sell off land as their income decreased and, after the death of 'squire' Henry in 1920, the hall was rarely occupied.

Not wishing to see them melted down, the gates were removed by a local builder, Arthur Walsh, during the last war for safe keeping, however they have since disappeared! Only the name, Marple Hall Drive, gives any clue to the origin of the road.

Stockport Road, Rose Hill, Marple.   No. 2.

The railway line, running from Marple Wharf Junction to Macclesfield, was opened in 1869. Trains ceased to run beyond the Rose Hill Station in 1970. The Railway Inn was built in 1879, ten years after the line was completed, and was owned by Hannah Arrowsmith, who also owned the Ring of Bells pub by the Macclesfield Canal on Church Lane.

Now that the Bowling Green and the Jolly Sailor have gone there are no public houses between the Navigation Inn, by the Peak Forest Canal at the top of Stockport Road, and the Railway. Also gone is the old signpost on the left of the photograph that indicated the way to the 'Cripples Hospital'. Modernised in recent years The Railway, like almost every other pub, serves food.

Norbury Smithy was the old name for the area around the Texaco Garage. The smithy, one of three that used to be in the hamlet, is the old building beyond the two shops on the left of the photograph, taken in the 1920s. The Bowling Green public house can be seen beyond the smithy. It was established in 1790 when Marple was changing from an area of scattered hamlets to a mill village, and remained open until 2000.

Left empty after some trouble finding a tenant, vandals broke in and started a fire which destroyed the building on the 11th of September 2001, a date that is seared into the memory of everyone. A photographer was on hand to record the event. Now demolished, the site has been used for new terraces of houses

with the name Windsor Court. What a shame the new name does not relate to the previous use of the site. Bowling Green Court sounds good to the authors!

Stockport rd. Marple

The scene of this beautifully clear picture of the junction of Stockport Road, Station Road and Church Lane in the early 1900s has changed dramatically. It now has traffic lights, pedestrian islands, road markings and an almost constant stream of cars, buses and lorries.

The Jolly Sailor was built in 1835 and had a very successful and busy place in village life. A stop for coaches and a place for societies to hold functions, it had a bowling green and was the venue for Marple's first post office. It has been closed for many months, its future uncertain; probably demolition.

A Methodist Sunday School was licensed for public worship in the cellar of one of the cottages next to the public house in 1795. They were demolished in the slum clearances of the 1930s and the empty area was used for many years as a site for a travelling fair. The big tree and the houses behind it have also gone and the setts have disappeared under tarmac.

A nother postcard of an empty Stockport Road in the early 1900s. The photographers often deliberately chose a time of the day when there would be no traffic. Sunny Bank Terrace, on the right, was built in 1868. This handsome row of six houses, with the corner one always used as a shop or café, has changed very little - the houses are still sought after and a shoe shop now occupies the corner. The large tree on the opposite side of the road survived until the 1950s.

The signpost has long since disappeared as has the large Hollins Mill, which stood just beside it. The site is now occupied by the Hollins row of shops, a supermarket and a large car park. There are now traffic lights, pedestrian crossings and the liberal application of yellow and white road markings everywhere.

Hollins Terrace, a row of ten houses with small front and back gardens, still stands but there is no longer a view from the front windows across a field. Now they look out on the telephone exchange and apartments for the retired. The terrace was built by the owners of Hollins Mill, for their employees. Not very far to walk to work and definitely within hearing distance of the factory hooter! The mill site is now occupied by the Coop superstore.

There were three rows originally, two rows of smaller homes were demolished at different times to provide space for the fire station and car park. Hollins Terrace with its larger houses was probably for the mill overlookers. At some time the end house by Hollins Lane was demolished and the front gables were lost. The back walls were totally rebuilt in recent years. In the new photo, taken of the back of the houses, the edge of the telephone exchange can just be seen.

Only the Bulls Head in Market Street at the end of the street remains today from the buildings shown in this very early photograph of the late 1890s. The first Marple Co-op store took over the shops along the left side of the street in 1874. Above the shops can be see the roof of the large Primitive Methodist Chapel, demolished in April 1964. The very old cottages, Linn Row, behind the chapel were demolished earlier. The small shop on the right was replaced by a building used by the Marple Urban District Council before they moved to the War Memorial Park. It was then used as Vernons furniture store, later it became the District Bank, now the National Westminster.

Today the first and second Co-op stores have gone whilst the third is currently occupied by McKays clothes shop. The street was pedestrianised in the early 1970s. The latest additions to this street scene are the cameras installed to record and hopefully deter the activities of local vandals!

L ocal postcard photographers liked to include some winter scenes in their stock. This one by Sharples, a prolific producer of local pictures, was taken looking up Stockport Road towards the Peak Forest Canal around 1905. Very little has changed! The tall building is now a flower shop, and just this side of it is the building occupied by an Italian restaurant. At the beginning of the last century it was James Lee's ironmongers shop, whose stock included gunpowder. Following an explosion one of Mr Lee's sons was tragically killed and extensive damage caused to the building.

On the left is the entrance to Hollins Mill, beyond it was the Union Rooms, which sold tea and included a library and mission hall. It was built by Thomas Carver, one of the owners of the mill, to provide an alternative to the many public houses in the village. For many years now it has been the home of The Regent Cinema, one of very few remaining independent cinemas in the country!

What a contrast between the two photographs, one from the 1950s and the other today. From absolute dereliction to desirable residence!

The toll cottage was built to collect money on the transfer of goods to and from the canal to Wharf Road, since renamed St Martins Road. Whilst the sixteen canal locks were under construction a tram way was used to transport goods between the two ends of the canal at Top Lock and the Aqueduct, part of its route along Wharf Road. The transformation is down to one man's determination that this lovely building shouldn't be lost. After years of hard work renovating the property he now has a house that is the envy of many people.

The market hall plans were vetoed by Stockport and the building was then used for housing. The big house behind the cottages, Beechwood, was built for Edward Ross, secretary for the railway company.

In 1936/7 Stone Row was demolished under the slum clearance scheme. If only they had survived for another fifty years and been modernised they would now be highly desirable! In their place a close of houses and bungalows was built. Beechwood House used recently as a nursing home, is now apartments. In the picture, *c.* 1910, many of the occupants have come out to watch the photographer. The motorbike and sidecar are without doubt amongst the earliest of these vehicles; the first was manufactured around 1885.

Samuel Oldknow's large Mellor Mill was working by 1792, and his many activities included the building of houses for his workers. Stone Row was not a row but two lines of back to back cottages, with occupied cellars, which were joined at one end by a section originally designed as a Market Hall.

Brentwood House on Church Lane still exists, extended and renamed McNair Court, with apartments for retired people. It was built around the turn of the last century and was occupied for many years by Harry Bickerton and family. He is famous for being one of the first to realise the potential of the diesel engine. The postcard dates from his time, as typed on the back is an invitation for a works employee to a function at the house. Later a Colonel and Mrs McNair lived in the house. They are remembered in Marple mainly for the gift of the swimming baths.

In 1937 the house, then called Brentwood, became a residential, recuperative and training centre for families under stress, mostly from inner city areas. During the war years this work ceased and the home was used for women and children who had lost their homes in bombing raids. The home, reopened after the war, closed in 1970.

This post card is of great interest because it shows Hibbert Lane with Goyt Mill under construction in the early 1900s. The mill was completed by 1905 but not fully equipped until 1912. In the 1930s there were around 480 employees. With the recession in cotton manufacturing the mill closed after the last war. It was subsequently used for some years to make plastic foam. Now sub-divided into separate units it survives, but without its chimney, which was felled in the 1980s. The photograph shows a very quiet Hibbert Lane with the photographer-watchers wearing an assortment of hats, most of which would have been made in the towns nearby.

The road is now busy with traffic and cluttered with parked cars but the cottages and mill still remain.

A small green in Hawk Green but not THE Green, in the early 1900s. The triangle of grass still remains with the addition of some trees on the opposite side of the road to the Green. The gap on the left of the road in the centre of the picture has been filled with houses. The cottages on the far left were demolished and replaced with a new terrace, whilst the space between the houses on the right was filled with more houses. The road leads to Barnsfold, a group of farms and cottages whose origins go back before Norman times.

Just how many copies of this postcard would have sold? It could almost qualify for a 'most boring' entry.

HAWK GREEN, MARPLE,

great deal of the attractive scenery has been saved.

In between the cottages can be seen the Ridge Methodist Church. Used first as a schoolroom it was built on the site in 1843 at the cost of £100. Later it was enlarged to be used a church and Sunday school. In 1874 an enormous new chapel was built beside the original. It can be seen on the ridge in the photo on page 68. Nicknamed the 'Cathedral of the North' it was demolished in recent years. The original chapel, used as a Sunday school when the large building was in use, is now again the chapel.

The modern photograph shows one of the most notable differences between houses then and now, the removal of chimney stacks.

A scene that has changed very little over the century since the photograph was taken. Marple grew tremendously in the 1960s and 70s. In one year in the sixties over 400 private houses were built! Due to the placing of a 'Green Belt' around the area in 1955 a

The photograph shows crowds out celebrating in Marple Bridge. The reason for the occasion is unknown.

Marple Bridge was given its name when the local fords were replaced, first by a bridge taking horses and people and then with a cart bridge in the early 1600s. The River Goyt marked the boundary between Derbyshire and Cheshire until 1936 when the townships of Mellor and Ludworth were made part of Marple Urban District, much to their disgust! In the nineteenth century many Irish lived in the area and indeed it was known as a 'rough place', a place to move out of, not to move into as nowadays!

Chapter 2

MARPLE BRIDGE
AND BRABYNS
BROW

Brabyns Brow during the First World War, and the scene has scarcely changed at all. The cobbles have been replaced by tarmac and many road signs have been erected, but the walls and Brabyns Lodge, at one of three entrances to Brabyns Hall, remain. The two figures walking down the road are soldiers dressed in uniforms which denote that they have been wounded in the Great War. They would have been returning down the hill to Brabyns Hall, which was being used as a military hospital.

Over the years there have been many accidents on the Brow, with horses, bicycles, lorries and cars. In 1851 a horse bolted with the gig containing a local mill owner and his wife; she was thrown from the cart and was so badly injured she subsequently died.

The photograph shows the arrival of a wounded soldier at the front door of Brabyns Hall during the First World War. Soldiers would be transported from the Front to England and then on to one of the many military hospitals set up all over the country in large private houses and public buildings. Brabyns Hall was used as a military hospital from the outbreak of war when the owner, Miss Hudson, offered its use to the Red Cross. It continued as such until May 1919, having helped countless soldiers both local and foreign to recuperate from their wounds.

When Miss Hudson died in 1941 at the age of ninety, her will gave the local councils the option of buying Brabyns Estate, excluding the Hall. The councils

bought the land for around £11,100 in 1943. In 1949 the Hall was purchased, it was hoped for use as a community centre, but the building was said to be in such bad structural condition that it was demolished in 1952. The site is now a car park!

The cottages at the bottom of Brabyns Brow in the early 1900s and today. It is very difficult for people today to believe the cottages in the two photos are the same buildings. In the early years of the last century there were many accidents involving lorries crashing into the houses and shops. There was a very sharp bend around the edge of Dr Hibbert's house, on the right of the picture. In the early 1930s the bridge was widened and the doctors house along with the two cottages closest to the river demolished. The new straightened road allowed the remaining cottages to have front gardens! Now of course there are traffic lights at the bottom of the hill. The distinctive 'gothic' windows of one of the cottages remain. The cottages were part of Brabyns Hall estate.

The hillside visible at the back of the old picture was farmland. With the building of the Constable Drive Estate and St Mary's Roman Catholic Primary School the fields no longer remain!

Marple Bridge Corn Mill, another of Marple's lost buildings. The water powered corn mill in the picture of the early 1900s was built in 1691 but it replaced an earlier medieval one, first recorded in 1354. In 1857 it had two wheels and five pairs of grinding stones, along with a drying kiln and stables. Disused by the 1930s, it was later demolished. The level of the weir was lowered in 1962 because of the foam caused by the pollution of the River Goyt. That problem having now been solved, a new mill pond would look very good. The old corn mill would have made good apartments, a small hotel or a very good restaurant!

The old wheel pit and wall can still just be seen across the river but trees have grown on the site. The level of the river was much higher until the Goyt Reservoirs higher up the valley were constructed.

Town Street, Marple Bridge

The new photo shows the buildings looking much the same as the photo taken in the early 1970s but the street scene very different. On the night of the 21 December 1991, after heavy rain, a large section of the river wall collapsed taking half the road and the gas main with it. For a year Town Street was impassable to traffic, whilst a completely new wall was built further out into the river, thus widening the road at a cost of over a million pounds.

The type of shops on Town Street has changed greatly. At the time of the photograph there was, amongst others, a delicatessen, a greengrocers, two butchers, a bakers and a dress shop; none of these now exist. Their places have been taken by antique shops, estate agents and hairdressers, however the Post Office remains, still run by the same family. The doctor's practice remains on Town Street but now is in what was Congregational Sunday school (see page 32).

Some changes have taken place in Town Street from seventy years ago, but not too many. The overall shape of the buildings remains the same but with many new windows and blinds. The Railway has a new front and has been renamed the Royal Scot much to the puzzlement of the local people. It was puzzling when it was called the Railway Hotel or Tavern in the 1830s, as it was thirty-five years before the railway reached Marple! It is still a Robinson's of Stockport establishment, holding a special place in the brewery's history having been their very first pub! Outside the building stands a horse and cart, its owner was inside supping 'Robbies' best. Doubtless later the horse would have known its way home without help from the driver.

Town Street, Marple Bridge

The photograph must have been taken in winter from the top of the steep bank that rises from the River Goyt opposite Town Street, Marple Bridge. Hollins Lane can be seen winding up the hill on its way to Mill Brow. It was part of the original road to Glossop before parts of the Glossop Road were built when it became a turnpike in 1802.

On the left hand corner of the road is the large Congregational Sunday school, now a doctors surgery, with the church on the land above it. Behind that church, a little further up the road, are St Mary's Roman Catholic church and school. On the right at the start of Hollins Lane can be seen a row of cottages that used to stand by the stream that comes down from Mill Brow. They were demolished many years ago and the car park now stands in their place.

The vast increase in the number of trees in last hundred years means that this view is now only possible framed by branches and leaves.

When Samuel Oldknow's Mellor Mill burnt down in 1892 the mill ponds and surrounding land were taken over by the manager, renamed the 'Roman Lakes', and run as a tourist attraction. The area attracted thousands of people, works outings, Sunday school treats, societies celebrations, etc. Most arrived at Marple Station from the surrounding towns on special trains and then walked to the Lakes. Many by way of Low Lea Road as can be seen in this photograph. There were boats for hire, penny slot machines and tea rooms.

The scene remains almost the same today and the area around the Roman Lakes is still an attraction with boating and refreshments. Special trains are not run anymore and people arrive by car and not in the thousands they used to until the 1950s!

The scene is hardly recognisable today, not helped by the growth of so many trees. From the days of the photograph, taken in the early 1900s, there have been many changes. The farm building on the right has gone, replaced by a road.

Marple Bridge Gas Works stood behind the inside of the bend of Lower Fold. A small works, it was started in 1845 by James Platt, and was later taken over by a company. Marple Council bought it in 1925 and later extended the works. The premises and a large gasometer that dominated the area were demolished in 1976. The site has since been used for residential development. Through the trees in the modern photograph Ludworth School can be seen. It was built by Derbyshire Council in 1907, the first purpose built council school in the area.

The Iron Bridge was constructed in 1813 by Salford Iron Works for the then owner of the Brabyns Estate, Nathaniel Wright. It would have been transported from Salford to Marple in sections aboard horse drawn carts and on arrival would have been pieced together like a giant jigsaw puzzle. The bridge gave Wright and successive owners a direct route from the hall to Compstall. In 1991 the local council declared it unsafe and placed a 'Bailey Bridge' over the Iron Bridge to temporarily 'protect it'. Thirteen years on with the temporary bridge still in situ and the Iron Bridge in a very sorry condition there is an ongoing campaign to restore it to its former glory. Efforts

are being made to obtain money from the Lottery Heritage Initiative which could provide funding for the bridge to be included as part of an educational and recreational project.

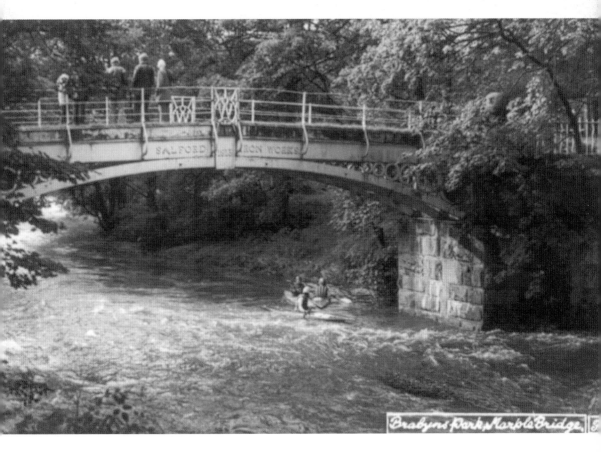

35

be demolished to avoid the cost of
bringing services to the streets and
modernising the houses. Thank
goodness that was avoided! Later, after
much debate, the mill estate was
purchased by the local council, and is
now the extremely popular Etherow
Country Park.

The picture was taken looking down
on cottages, now demolished, to where
the entrance to the park now stands.
The row of terraced houses in the
centre of the picture remains as does the
'Athenaeum', the building just behind
them. It was built by the Andrews for
the use of the village and was used in
recent years as a library and meeting
place. Now that the library is closed it is
hoped to use part of the building as a
local history centre.

Compstall village was built during
the late 1700s by the Andrews
family, for the workers in their large
cotton mills. Manufacturing by
successive owners continued until 1966.
In the 1950s there was the strong
possibility that the entire village would

The post office, near the recreation ground on Longhurst Lane in the 1920s. This was the second position for the Mellor Post Office. Its final position was in Moor End but it closed in 1995. With the finish a few years later of the Mellor News shop, which was further down Longhurst Lane, there are now no shops between New Mills and Marple Bridge.

In the 1800s and early 1900s you did not need to leave Mellor for any purchase! There was a co-op and a bank and nearly all shops had a delivery service. Today the weekly run to the supermarket has taken over, leaving difficulties for those without transport, the elderly and the young. There is an infrequent bus service and even this does not run in the evenings, on a Sunday or Bank Holidays! A recent change has seen the Marple co-op delivery service start again after a break of many years.

Chapter 3
MELLOR AND
MILL BROW

These cottages on Low Lea Road have been modernised since the photograph was taken in the early 1900s. Bow windows have been inserted, and the buildings extended. In 1891 there were six houses with thirty adults and children living in them. Now the occupants are far less in number and the houses have cars parked outside. The road however looks as if it was in better condition a century ago.

A family called Riley are outside their cottage in 1909, was it a special occasion? The back of the photograph gives the names of the three generations. The man in the centre of the picture holding a child is Jack Riley, in the modern photograph are his grandson and great grandson Jack and Kevin Frogatt (and Ben).

Townscliffe farm probably goes back to before the Norman Conquest but no documents survive from that time. In the nineteenth century a family named Lees, gentlemen and property owners in Hyde, lived there. The photograph dates from before the First World War.

The cottage and some of the land was used as a very hilly nine-hole golf course before the First World War. The club ceased to function around 1920 and the members were absorbed into the Mellor Club, which still has its course on Cobden Edge. The name is still perpetuated in its title of the 'Mellor and Townscliffe Golf Club'.

There was an application in the early seventies for a housing development on the adjoining fields but this was rejected! The barns, but not the farm or attached cottage, then came up for auction. They were then converted into three houses. The lovely 'gothic' window of the barn is no longer visible and the styles of the conversions not particularly 'Pennine'.

Methodists held meetings and ran a Sunday School in late 1700s in the first cottage on the right. After they moved to New House Hill Chapel in the 1840s the rooms were used as a Sunday school by Mellor Church, thus the name of the cottages, 'School Row'. The sharp bend at the other end of the road was eliminated by the demolition of the last house. In the middle of the picture can be seen the new bungalow, one of the first of the 'ribbon development' of Longhurst Lane, in the first half of the last century.

Today School Row is still recognisable, despite window changes. The view on the other side of the road is totally different. In 1912 a scout drill hall was erected which was replaced by the new Sports Club in 1984. The Conservative club was built on the adjoining plot in 1911. Chadwick's builders yard was next to the cottages, now used for renovation of classic cars. A new house has also been squeezed in.

A holiday home for mothers and children from the centre of Manchester was first established in Gibb Lane in the late 1800s. The purpose-built Manchester Cathedral Home on Longhurst Lane was opened in 1909. Originally there was a wind pump in the adjoining field for raising water from a well. Mellor did not get piped water until 1926. The home is still used for holiday accommodation and financed by money given by the public.

The old picture shows the home just built. There are no curtains at the windows and the drive has recently been gravelled. The new photograph shows once again how many trees have grown in the last hundred years.

Devonshire Arms Mellor

Built in around 1817, the photograph shows The Devonshire during the time it was a Bells & Co. house. Bells were bought out in 1949 by the Frederick Robinson Brewery, who still own the pub. The wall at the front of the building has gone and a porch now covers the original doorway. The bus timetable can be seen on the wall.

From the outside the Devonshire Arms doesn't look very different today, however, these days nearly every public house serves food and the 'Devi' is no exception. To cater for this trade there is now a large car park beside the building and a garden area out the back. When renovations were carried out a few years ago the original well was discovered at the rear.

This view has not changed substantially in nearly a century, although most of the windows have been changed. Lower Hall, on the hillside top-right, now has a 'gothic' look. The house was home to several generations of the Jowetts, who owned collieries and a great deal of land in Mellor and the surrounding area for over two hundred years. In the nineteenth century nearly a tenth of local working men were coal miners. In 1851 there were fifty-one adults and children in the hamlet on census night! In one cottage alone there were nine children aged from twelve to sixteen, all born in Ireland! They all worked in the cotton mills. Next door was Thomas Waller, cotton spinner and manufacturer, his father was one of the owners of Dove Bank Mills in Moor End. The Irish youngsters probably

worked in the Waller's mill. Now the houses, almost all modernised, are occupied by commuters. The cottage that shows its gable end has been extended over the stream.

The bottom of Church Road was a new road at the time of the photograph. In 1893 Jonas Craven of Mellor Hall and Jonathan Jowett of Lower Hall co-operated in building a 'by-pass' to Brookbottom. Previously the only way up to the church, school, houses and farms on the hillside had been the steep and stony way through Brookbottom. The new road had an iron gate at the Longhurst Lane end, which was closed and padlocked for one day every year to preserve its private status.

In the photograph the fields and walls look well kept. The new villas on Gibb Lane can be seen in the centre of the picture; they were constructed using the stone of the derelict Dove Bank Mills in Moor End.

Now there are more houses on Longhurst Lane and Gibb Lane The barn at the end of the group in the foreground is now a house but the scene has changed little. There are more trees and the walls are not so well maintained.

The old picture of Mellor School was taken in the first decade of the last century. The school, originally a church one, had been built in 1880, to replace a single room one in the churchyard. The old building still exists with extensions added over the years by the school authorities. Modern teaching methods and the severe lack of space inside and outside led to a campaign for a new school. In the 1990s the pupils moved into a brand new school built further down Longhurst Lane. The land was given by the Arkwrights for educational purposes and lengthy negotiations with the descendants of the family had to be undertaken to get permission to use the buildings as a Parish Centre. The buildings, owned by the church and empty for four years,

have now been extensively modernised to become the Parish Centre with facilities for everything from conferences to children's parties.

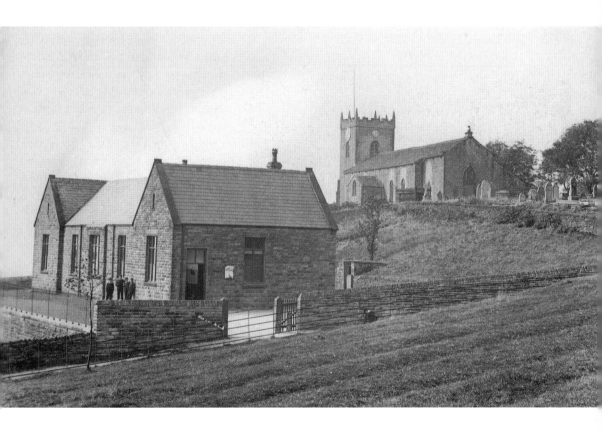

MELLOR CHURCH

The north side of Mellor Church. The tower of the church dates from the fifteenth century but it is possible that there was an earlier building. In the 1990s it was discovered by archaeologists that the hilltop had been used as an Iron Age fort and later occupied by the Romans. Flints from the Mesolithic Age were also found. The site has been occupied for over 10,000 years!

Open days have been held for the last three years attracting hundreds of people. They come to see the year's excavations, finds and displays. The photograph shows two young archaeologists standing in the bottom of the section of the ditch dug in the first millennium BC. This 'hole' is left open, other excavations are back-filled each season.

The dip in the road in the centre of the picture is where the stream that flows to Marple Bridge lies. For most of its course the stream is the boundary between Mellor and Ludworth, and its water powered several cotton mills in the late nineteenth and early twentieth centuries.

However the boundary between the townships includes some land on the other side of the stream as the caption on the postcard of the early 1900s records 'Hollywood End, Mellor' not Mill Brow, Ludworth.

Sycamore Farm is in the centre of the picture. Blacksmiths named Wood occupied the farm for many years thus giving it its original name of Blacksmiths Farm. No longer a farm, the house was modernised some years ago and now the barn is being converted to another home, a common story in the area today. With no further need for such barns, permission is often granted for conversions, which albeit controversial, do save the buildings from dereliction or demolition.

HollyWood End Mellor

B.P.C.

47

The pub was built, *c*. 1810 and the adjoining cottages were incorporated into the pub when modernisation took place some time early last century. In the valley below the Hare and Hounds lies Holly Vale. The area included, in the century before last, three cotton mill buildings, a warehouse, a gas works, four rows of cottages, two houses and a farm. The mills have long gone and the dwellings, now modernised, are highly desirable and expensive. There were also coal mines and quarries in the area, quite enough people to patronise the pub. Now the Hare and Hounds, complete with seventies bow window, serves food as well as Robinsons beers to locals, walkers and car occupants alike.

Ron Giles climbs the ladder at the raising of the wooden cross on Cobden Edge by Marple Council of Churches in 1970. The planning application to place the cross on the Edge was opposed by some local people. In the background one can just make out Goyt Mill complete with the chimney that was knocked down some years later.

St Thomas' Church began in early medieval times as a chapelry in the enormous Parish of Glossop in the Diocese of Lichfield; now St Thomas' is a parish in its own right in the Diocese of Derby. Marple had no chapel of its own until the 1500s; it was part of the large Parish of Stockport, also for many centuries in the Diocese of Lichfield. Now All Saints Church is in the Diocese of Chester.

The churches were an all-pervading part of the lives of the people up until recent times. They controlled every aspect of people's everyday movements. The Anglican churches since the times of Elizabeth I were the 'local government' of the day, looking after the roads, policing, the poor etc. Baptisms, marriages and burials of course were conducted in the church.

Chapter 4
CHURCHES AND SCHOOLS

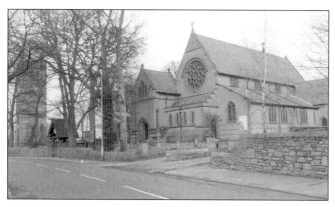

The two All Saints Churches, Georgian and Victorian, in the early years of the last century. Although a wooden chapel had been built on the Ridge for the people of Marple in the 1500s, a bench was still set aside for them in St Mary's Stockport in the 1600s. The church, in a decrepit state, was blown down by a gale in 1804. Samuel Oldknow led the campaign and contributed greatly to the building of the Georgian Church, completed by 1812. When later in the century the structure was found too weak to allow for the construction of a new aisle a completely new church was built alongside the old, consecrated in 1872. In 1959 all of Oldknow's church except the tower was demolished.

The Victorian church was altered internally to allow for modern and different forms of worship in the late 1970s. The bells in the tower of the Georgian church still ring out over the countryside.

All the churches and chapels in the district had 'Whit Walks' in the late nineteenth and the first half of the twentieth centuries. The picture from the first decade of the last century shows All Saints Sunday school processing down Stockport Road. Almost every child attended a Sunday school and each year the school would parade through the town with their banners held high. The procession has so many people in it that the column reaches back to Hollins Mill. There is no traffic on the road at all, did the churches have to obtain 'road closure orders'? The volume of traffic is so great these days, even on public holidays, that the closing Stockport Road would not be allowed.

There are no Whit Walks these days. Members of the churches of the district

walk up to the cross on Cobden Edge on Good Friday and St Thomas' congregation led by the choir, walk up Church Road on Palm Sunday. The modern photograph is taken from the same position!

Mellor has had Rose Queens, with a few breaks, for over seventy years. Crowned at the Church Fete in June, she and her attendants raise money throughout the year for a local charity.

The fete was held until 1999 on the Church field, Longhurst Lane, and is now held on the top of the hill by the Church. The field, acquired in the first few years of the last century, was recently sold for housing, a very controversial planning decision strongly attacked by some local residents. The money raised has been used to modernise and change the old empty Mellor School into a Parish Centre. The old school closed when the new one was opened in 1997 half way down Longhurst Lane, again a controversial change.

The old photograph shows the crowning of Thelma Jowett as 'Queen' in 1937. The modern photograph was taken at Marple Carnival of last years 'Queen' Jennifer Dayes and her Rosebuds on one of the floats.

The first Methodist Church on Church Lane was built on land purchased from Ottiwell Higginbotham for £25 in around 1804 and in 1812 a Methodist Sunday school, seen in the picture, was built. Both were rebuilt in the late nineteenth century into the building. In 1964/65, having combined with the Trinity Methodists, additional rooms were added to both buildings, and a new common frontage, using stone from the demolished Trinity Chapel on Market Street, was constructed.

Today this thriving church is still very much in use and in addition to the Methodists, many organisations and clubs meet in and use the halls.

A group of Primitive Methodists first met in a cottage at Step Houses on Chatterton Lane and after several moves built a chapel on Gird Lane above Mill Brow in 1875; rebuilding it in 1906. The photograph shows the chapel in its final years around the late 1960s. The workers from the cotton and bleaching mills on the stream, along with coal miners and quarry workers, worshipped in the chapel. By the 1960s with the decline in population and the end of nearly all local sources of employment the chapel closed.

By the 1980s old mill workers cottages were being bought by commuters for renovation. The semi-derelict state of Mill Brow and Holly Vale in the 1930s can scarcely be imagined by the people who live in the hamlet today. The chapel was converted into a home but the exterior remains almost unaltered to remind passers by of its original use.

The Carver brothers and Samuel and William Hodgkinson, partners in the Hollins Mill, were the leaders in the establishing of the Congregational Church in Marple, which opened in 1864. Thomas Carver however, soon left the church to open his own multi denominational Union Rooms next to the Mill. Both families were also the leaders in the building of the Albert Sunday school on Church Lane.

The church is now called the United Reformed; the Congregational and Presbyterian denominations having come together in recent years. The spire was removed in 1939 due to structural faults.

Today, with its widened carriageway and busy traffic, Hibbert Lane is a very different road. The building of the first

secondary school for boys in the district in 1931 was followed by housing for the elderly, and both council and private estates changed the road completely. A very different community on that side of Marple to that of the 1860s. This is about the only modern photograph in the book showing fewer trees than the old one.

A class photograph inside the Albert Schools on Church Lane, before 1900, of twenty boys and girls, probably five or six years old. There were no school uniforms then and arms were tightly folded for the photograph. It appears to be a model-making lesson, in sand and clay. The pupils came from families who worked in the mills or on the land.

The school was established in 1868 and the building used for Sunday and day education, by the Congregational Church on nearby Hibbert Lane. Children at this time left school around twelve years old and it was said that if you attended Albert Schools, you had a better chance of getting a job at Hollins Mill. The mill was owned by the Carvers and Hodgkinsons who were strong Congregationalists!

The buildings today are used by an overall making company and the inside is little changed apart from the replacing of desks by sewing machines.

A photograph of All Saints boys in 1928. The names of the boys are not known; however, looking very smart in their jackets, jumpers and ties they, if alive, would now be in their seventies. Not enough for a class photograph, perhaps they were a football team.

All Saints School started its life on the upper floor of a barn at Chapel House Farm in 1831. It moved to its present site in 1838 on land given by Richard Arkwright. Some money had to be paid to attend the school in order to pay the schoolmaster or mistress. The school was completely rebuilt in 1902 and extended further in the1960s. It is a church school and this year is celebrating the centenary of its 'new" school. The modern photograph shows a group of today's children at the same school.

A class at Ludworth School in the early 1900s and the contrast with one of today in the very same classroom. The school was built by Derbyshire County Council in 1907, in their favoured 'bungalow' style' in stone with a rustic tiled roof. It was the first school built by a council in the area. It opened with one hundred and four children. There were boys, and girls yards and the toilets were at the far end of the playing areas! From 1926 onwards it was also used as a school for senior children of Mellor and Ludworth, that being children above the age of eleven, as Derbyshire had no secondary school in the area. This ceased in 1936 when Ludworth and Mellor were 'transferred' from Derbyshire to Cheshire, and the scholars went to the Willows on Hibbert Lane in Marple.

All the original school buildings are still in use with the addition of new classrooms, a hall and entrance in the last thirty years.

Not a good quality photograph, but one that is too good not to use. The band playing outside the Pineapple on Market Street, around the beginning of the last century, is probably Marple Band.

The Pineapple originally had it's front door on Church Lane but in 1892 the pub was demolished and re-built with the main entrance placed on, the now more important, Market Street. In 1936/7 The Pineapple were winners of the very first Marple and District Dart and Dominoes League, a competition that they still contest fiercely to this day.

Chapter 5
CELEBRATION
AND
ENTERTAINMENT

The Coronation [?] 22 [?] 1911. Singing God Save the King. 91[?]

In this Golden Jubilee year in the reign of Queen Elizabeth II it is interesting to compare the celebrations with those for the Coronation of George V in June 1911. The district had flags flying in the streets and Mellor had a day of processions, children's activities, picnics and a bonfire on Cobden Edge. The main events took place in the field now used by the Sports Club. Each child received a mug. The post card has the title 'singing God Save the King' but the crowd does not appear to be singing or indeed paying any attention to the man examining the piece of paper on the stand.

The main local celebrations this year centred around Hawk Green with three days of events ranging from a charity cricket match to karaoke on the Green, competitions and a tug-of-war! Despite the weather not smiling on the events a great community spirit prevailed.

People celebrating the Coronation of Queen Elizabeth II in 1953 next to the council offices in the War Memorial Park. It was the first time that a Coronation had appeared on television, not that many people owned one. The weather was windy and wet, a situation that was repeated for the Queen's Golden Jubilee celebrations. In 2002 the dancing was somewhat less formal and the main venue had moved up the road to Hawk Green but a good time was had by all none the less.

A photograph of Marple's Home Guard in the years of the Second World War. In the early 1940s when there was the threat of a German invasion the Local Defence Volunteers were formed as a first line of defence in protecting Britain's shores. Locally, weapons and ammunition were hidden down a well close to the Old Vicarage, Mellor, in order to arm a resistance force should they fail. A young man living in the house was a member of Mellor's Home Guard and recommended the hiding place. In 1996 the well was opened for the first time since the removal of most of the weapons at the end of the war. Still down the well was a very corroded American Tommy Gun and further exploration of the well last year ended with a bucket full of live ammunition! John and Ann Hearle are seen displaying the gun just after it had been retrieved from the well!

The Marple Carnival has its origins back in the early years of the last century but after a number of years and for reasons unknown it folded. It was started again in 1962, meaning that this year (2002) it celebrated the fortieth anniversary of it's rebirth.

The early photograph is of the 1905 carnival and shows the procession turning out of Bowden Lane and setting off up Stockport Rd. The Police station on the left hand corner remains today albeit a portion of the garden has been lost to road widening. Over the years the route of the carnival has changed many times, at the time of the old photograph the starting place was probably on the fields that are now the Norbury Drive estate. The modern

photo shows Marple Band starting the 2002 procession ably supported by Marple's firemen.

HIBBERT LANE MARPLE ROMAN SERIES COPYC 75L

these days, with all the through traffic and all the coming and going from Ridge Danyers Sixth Form College. Just who was the dapper man at the end of the row? The shop front at the back of the photograph was Charles William Burgess, grocer. From the directories we know that the shop was already there in 1910 and still remained in 1923. There are no grocery stores on Church Lane now.

In the 1970s an extension of Hibbert Lane to Stockport Road was constructed. Now a busy roundabout stands on the spot behind the policemen and the shop is occupied by Littlewoods, the butchers. The modern photograph shows the staff of the veterinary practice that has been in the last house on the left for many years.

Marple's local police force in Hibbert Lane before the First World War. Four substantial men, well capable of 'clipping' a young lad's ear when caught misbehaving. You would not stand in the middle of Hibbert Lane

Stone from the old township quarry on the Ridge was used to build many of the houses in Marple. By the early part of the last century, brick had become the main building material and the quarry was used for a number of years as a venue for concerts to raise money for local charities. It was also a popular picnic area. The people in the photograph, taken in the early 1900s, were in their Sunday best and all seem to be watching the photographer whilst the band plays on. They would have been able to see the Peak Forest Canal and the old Strines Print Works below them with the hills of Mellor in the background.

The modern photograph shows that despite the provision of a car park and the many trees that have grown up in the last hundred years the view remains essentially the same.

OPEN AIR MUSICAL FESTIVAL AT RIDGE QARRY, MARPLE, 1909

Taken in 1967 this photograph of Mark Singleton was taken by an American magazine to illustrate life in Marple at the time when Mark and his family were heavily involved with the Marple band. Whilst the left-hand side of Chadwick Street (pictured) has remained virtually unchanged, the other side has completely altered having had all the buildings demolished. A large public car park and sheltered flats now occupy most of that side. Mark, (recreating his role in the modern photograph, along with the original baton) is now the licensee at the Hatters Arms in Marple and is still a keen supporter of the band.

Mellor Mill was one of the biggest of its time and employed over 500 men, women and children at its most productive. The fire that destroyed it in November 1892 left many unemployed in the days when there were no welfare benefits. If no money could be found, then the Stockport or New Mills Workhouses were the last resort for help.

After the fire destroyed Mellor Mill the old ponds that supplied the water to turn the three water wheels were used as a visitor attraction. Boats could be hired and many postcards were produced showing people boating. The one shown here is from the early 1900s. There were also tea-rooms, penny machines and in the thirties a dance floor. The area attracted thousands of people each weekend in the summer.

Brabyns Brow would be crowded morning and evening by people arriving and departing in their hundreds.

No longer visited by this volume of people, the site is still popular for fishing, boating and walking, refreshments can still be purchased.

The photograph of around the 1950s shows cricket being played on the green at Hawk Green, with the small club house and scoring hut visible behind the players. The game is no longer played on the green but on their 'new ground' in the village. Hawk Green's first pitch was near number three tee on Marple Golf Course, but in 1926 the Green was levelled to provide a playing place with a small pavilion on the corner of Windlehurst Road. The club moved to its present location in 1960. Marple and Mellor also have cricket grounds that are still well used, neither in their original locations. The very large Ridge Chapel can be seen on the hillside, it was demolished in the 1960s following the discovery of dry rot. The fields just behind the Green were built on around the same time.

The grounds of Rose Hill House, on which the Manchester Overspill houses were built after the last war, were lent to the Co-operative Society to hold a carnival in the early 1900s. The Victorian house, which can just be seen at the back of the photo, was demolished in the 1940s, and the road now called 'the Drive' was exactly that.

The Co-op in it's hey day could supply all the needs of the local people from supplying coal to arranging a funeral. As well as their local shops in Compstall, Marple Bridge, Mellor, Marple and Hawk Green, they delivered all their goods to the door. Most of the area's working people were members of the Society; some older people can still remember their 'divi' number.

One of the attractions for young people was the Punch and Judy show; today despite high tech special effects a pony ride is still a big draw.

PUNCH & JUDY SHOW
CO-OPERATIVE SOCIETY
CHILDRENS GALA
MARPLE

A fund raising, mixed cricket match at Hawk Green during the First World War to raise money for the war effort. Used as a post card the message on the back reads: 'These are a few of the people who played cricket the other Saturday. Our Phyllis did fine, she took six wickets for a very few runs, she also taught them how to hit boundaries. Don't you think they did well, £50, not bad for the boys.'

The teams seem to be made up of locals along with soldiers and sailors who must be on leave. The Crown today is still the focal point of many activities in Hawk Green.

The story of industry and transport in Marple is basically the story of Marple itself. From farming hamlets to a mill and mining small town. The chimneys of the mills dominated the skyline for over a hundred years. Then there were the canals, constructed to serve these industries, and on to the introduction of what was once the greatest railway system in the world, (the photograph above shows an LNER class C13 locomotive trapped at Rose Hill station in the winter of 1947).

Little of these are left, however the remaining mills provide accommodation for many small businesses and each year the canal traffic increases as Marple now becomes the focus of the tourism industry.

Chapter 6

INDUSTRY AND TRANSPORT

The Strines Hall Printing Company was started in 1792 and later became the Strines Print works in which machine printing was introduced. Although the works were in New Mills many of the people of Strines, Marple and Mellor worked for the company. In the 1850s there were several enlightened partners, who made the works a centre of cultural and educational life in the district. By the 1920s it was decided to build a new mill on the opposite side of the river and, whilst construction took place, business at the old mill continued. Once completed the old mill was demolished. The fact that both mills, including chimneys, can be seen dates the photo pretty accurately to the late twenties. After a number of crises in recent years the works closed down last year.

The building in the front of the picture was originally a storeroom for the works and later became the Sunday school for St Pauls, Strines. Before being demolished in 1972 it was used for a variety of other uses. The site is now occupied by houses.

In the centre of the photograph of Moor End, Mellor, dating from the early 1900s, is the chimney of Dove Bank Mills. The chimney was all that was left of the mills that dominated the village for almost a hundred years. Three brothers, Thomas, Ralph and Samuel Waller, cotton manufacturers in Manchester in the early 1800s, built a new mill in Moor End in the 1820s. Another large building was added later and most of the property and land around Moor End was acquired by the Wallers. The mills were burnt down in two fires in the 1870s leaving many people unemployed and the village in a distressed state. Thomas and Samuel were strong supporters of Methodism and built two chapels in Mellor. One is now a private house, the other the scout hut.

On the right is the Sunday school for Mellor Church, built in 1821. In the 1970s it was sold and converted to a house. Apart from the covered cobbles and no chimney, felled for road widening in 1929, the scene is readily recognisable today.

Stockport Road, Marple.

A photograph of Stockport Road in the early years of the last century. Hollins Mill, on the right, overshadowed the centre of Marple for over a hundred years. The first mills in the area were in Mellor and Ludworth and were water powered, but Hollins Mill, built in the 1830s by the Walmsley family, was steam driven. The firm later passed to the twin brothers Thomas and John Carver and their partners, the Hodgkinsons. The families had a tremendous impact on the district for around fifty years. The United Reformed Church on Hibbert Lane, the Union Rooms, the Working Men's Club, the Albert Schools, and the Boys Club were all their 'doing'. Their wives were the 'lady-bountifuls' of the area.

The factory passed through different owners and closed in 1956. The site is now occupied by the small Hollins shops, a car park and a supermarket. The Union Rooms are now the Regent Cinema, the Boys Club the Carver Theatre, and the Albert Schools a factory. The noise of the factory hooter and the machinery have been replaced today by the almost constant sound of traffic.

The photograph from the early 1900s shows the arm of the Peak Forest Canal, which was included in the construction of the Hollins Mill complex for the delivery and dispatch of goods straight into the factory yard. Thomas Carver with family and furniture arrived by boat to their new home and estate, now the Council Offices and the War Memorial Park. The canal arm was removed when the mill was demolished in the late 1950s. Thousands of people came to see the felling of the chimney, which can be seen at the back of the picture, in 1956. The chimney had towered over the centre of the village for many years.

The entrance to the canal arm can still be traced in the wall. The area around Possett Bridge (see page 2), was sponsored by the Civic Society, and was cleaned and made attractive with flowers and bushes under 'Operation Spring Clean'. The Queen viewed the site on her one and only visit to Marple in May 1981.

buildings were used for processing and grinding Plaster-of-Paris, lime and a high-sulphur coal. But fifty years later it had ceased working and had become derelict as can be seen in the photo taken in the early years of the last century.

The new photo shows that nothing remains of the buildings today except the roof of Bleak House which can be seen to the left of the mill. Fishing and boating are activities still to be found on the canal today. There is little commercial traffic now but since rescued from closure (the plan was to pipe the water and fill the canal with rubbish!) the canals are much used by leisure craft, both local and tourist.

Samuel Oldknow was not just a mill owner, he was involved in every aspect of life in the district. That included the construction of the Peak Forest Canal, the lime kilns and a mineral mill. By 1858 the mineral mill

The series of sixteen locks that raise the Peak Forest Canal from the Cheshire Plain to Marple were constructed in the first four years of the nineteenth century. They are one of Marple's 'tourist attractions' and its glory. The locks raise and lower boats, originally pulled along by horses, up over 200 feet, each lock having a rise of thirteen feet.

The old photo from the early 1900s compared with the modern shows few changes. Bungalows have been built along the far side of the canal. In sunshine or under cloud, there are always people walking the canal path, watching the boats or looking across to the Pennine hills. Kinder Scout, the highest place on the south of the Pennines at 2,000 feet, can easily be seen on a clear day. At the top lock, just off the photograph, the Macclesfield Canal starts and the area with its water, stone walls, bridges, boats and houses, old and new, attracts many visitors.

The Macclesfield Canal was one of the last canals to be built in the country. It was completed in 1831 and this photo of Marple Wharf, taken in the early 1900s, shows the Marple end. It linked the Peak Forest Canal and the Trent and Mersey Canals, and it provided a connection with the Potteries and the Midlands. The traffic along it declined with the arrival of the railways although some barges still worked until the after the last war. The photograph shows working boats and goods on the wharf.

The edge of the building just visible on the right was a warehouse for the transfer of goods under cover. Boats were able to moor inside the building. In the centre of the picture is one of the roving bridges on the canal, which allowed for horses to change to the other side of the water without being unhooked from the boat.

The scene has hardly changed, now there are few working barges and no cross bars on telegraph poles. The warehouse has been neglected in recent years and is in need of repair.

The entrance to Marple Station in the early 1900s. The Victorian buildings including the entrance were demolished in 1970. The station had been completed in 1864. In its heyday, following rebuilding around the 1890s, forty men and boys were employed, fifteen people on duty at any one time. With its four glass canopied platforms, waiting rooms, station master's house, goods yard and warehouse, it was 'main line standard'. There were direct services to Manchester, Stockport, Derby, Nottingham, Liverpool, London and many other major towns

Where the old entrance stood there is a flight of stairs down to the car park and a telephone box. The post box that was built into the entrance was not replaced.

The modern entrance is a very 'down market' affair, totally functional and architecturally nondescript! The goods yard is now the car park and is filled every day with local commuter's cars.

MARPLE STATION. 813.

Marple station in the days of steam. The platform buildings have all gone along with the goods yard. No longer do glass canopies keep the rain off the commuters! All the buildings were demolished and the new entrance block erected in their place. Only the bridge remains to show the former glory of the station. The modern photograph shows Manchester commuters awaiting their train.

In the early 1900s horse drawn carriages were used to deliver and collect the 'upper class merchants' who lived in the big houses of the area and commuted to Manchester and Stockport. The goods yard was very busy with coal deliveries and on Bank holidays literally thousands of people would pass through the station on their way to Roman Lakes and other local beauty spots.

A spectacular crash at Marple Bridge. It happened during the widening of the bridge on the downriver side in 1930. The driver of a lorry, full of bricks, lost control and broke through the old wall of the bridge. The crash immediately attracted a crowd of onlookers, mostly men. All the people, workers and public alike looked up for Garner, the local photographer, to take their picture. A North Western bus can be seen at the bus stop on Town Street.

The more modern picture shows the outcome of a five vehicle crash on the very same spot in April 1995. Nobody was badly injured, however firemen from Marple fire station had to use specialised cutting equipment to release one driver who was trapped.

proprietor of The Bulls Head on Market Street. Sadly, Tom's name is one of 141 names recorded on Marple War Memorial of local men killed in WW1. He was killed in action in Salonika on 31 March 1918. His brother, also in the army serving his country, had given his life the previous year in Mesopotamia.

Following the Great War J.T. Pott sold his taxi and funeral businesses to Malcolm Shaw, one of his competitors. The firm has remained in the Shaw family ever since and although the main part of the business concentrates on funerals, they are called occasionally upon to act as a taxi and take people to the airport. Pictured with today's limousine is Mark Shaw, grandson of Malcolm.

Tom Platt stands proudly in front of the car he chauffeured for William Dean of Lily Bank, Cobden Edge, Mellor. He also worked as a chauffer for J.T. Pott, who was the Chairman of Marple Urban District Council and

Not really a farm photograph, but the end of using the land for farming after numerous centuries. The first sod was cut for the start of a purpose built home for crippled children just off Dale Road in 1912 by Mrs C.B. Holmes. In 1907 the Manchester and Salford Cripples Help Society had taken a seven-roomed cottage on Cross Lane as a holiday Country Home. It was such a success that the new home was constructed on Dale Road for twenty four children.

In 1937 this became the Children's Orthopaedic Hospital for long-stay patients; whilst there they could continue their full-time education. Since the end of hospital use in 1981, the buildings have been used for respite care. Finally closed at the end of last year

Chapter 7
FARMS AND SHOPS

the site is to be redeveloped for housing.

Close by at Nab Top a nursing home was established in 1912. This grew to become a sanatorium for a hundred patients and in 1947 under the National Health system it took in many different categories of patients. The Dale hospital also closed in 1981 and is now a Nursing Home for the elderly. The old TB wards remain in a derelict state.

Stables Marple Hall

The Bradshaw Isherwoods of Marple Hall owned hundreds of acres in Marple and other parts of Cheshire. They were indeed minor gentry in the region. The arable land was used for cereals and root crops; there were fields for pasture and fields for growing hay. The big range of barns shown in the photograph of the early 1900s would have been used for storage and threshing. Nothing at all remains of the barns, stables and labourers cottages, demolished like the Hall, a tremendous loss for Marple.

On the site today stands Marple Hall School for children from eleven to sixteen. Only a date stone remains of the old hall, nothing of the outbuildings. The sundial is now in the War Memorial Park.

There are very few photographs of farming in the area. Like working in the mill, factory or shop, there are few photographs, nobody takes pictures of themselves at work. The old photograph, taken off Windlehurst Road in Hawk Green at the start of the last century, is one of only two known pictures of threshing in the area. The steam-powered machinery would probably have been rented for the days required, the expenditure on a piece a large piece of farm equipment would not have been justified for an individual farmer.

Few cereals were grown in the area during the last century. Earlier each farm would have sown some wheat, oats and barley, very little wheat was grown on the higher ground. The threshed grain would have been taken to the local corn mills. The one below Mill Brow was already in existence in the 1200s and that of Marple Bridge in the 1300s. The modern photograph shows the old grinding stone on the top of the Ludworth Mill dam today.

Most people today do not remember the widespread use of horses in farming. The horses in the photograph taken over a hundred years ago were ploughing fields on Cross Lane. Each farm would have its own ploughing team, the horses were also used for carting. The chimney of Hollins Mill can just be made out to the left of the man leading the horses. On the right of the picture is the spire that used to be on the United Reform Church on Hibbert Lane.

After the arrival of the tractor and the loss of farmland for housing the number of horses in the area declined greatly. However, recent years has seen their numbers increase due to the opening of several riding schools and there are many horses owned by individuals. Agriculture has been replaced by 'horsiculture'! The modern photograph shows children at Peacefield Primary School which now stands on the field in the old photograph.

The photograph shows a large building at The Dale Farm during the early part of the last century when it was used as a 'colony' to train young men in agriculture by the Christian Social Union. Refreshments could be obtained by walkers who would also be shown around the farm.

There were eighty-five dairy farms, many with large dairy herds in 1948 in the area. Until recently the farms Sunhill in Ludworth and the Dale in Marple still had milking herds. Conrad Clark of the Dale also delivered the farm's milk for many years around the village. People now mostly buy their milk in shops, not in the old glass bottles but in plastic or cardboard. The Dale has been sold in the last ten years and now has horses on the land. The old farm building still exists but is now put to residential use.

Knowle Farm, below Mellor Church, is still a working farm but of course no longer uses horses as in this photograph from the early part of the last century. Now there is no dairy herd but it keeps sheep in the winter and cattle in the summer for other farmers. Peter and John Hodgson, father and son, use their tractors on the farm and around the village to dig ditches, mend walls, cut hedges etc. They also use the tractor to help the archaeologists who dig each year by Mellor Church; Peter is examining the trench with his metal detector whilst John looks on!

The footpath to the church was used by people attending church services and by children attending Mellor School, and is still well used by ramblers. During the first half of the last century the footpaths of the district were well trodden by the thousands who left the nearby towns for the fresh air of the countryside.

This marvellous photograph from the first decade of the last century shows Gladys Pott, Phyllis and Lizzie Turner on their way to milking at Barnsfold Farm. In the background can be seen Barnsfold Manor house, one of the oldest houses in the Marple area dating back to before 1660.

Just look at the bonnets, the pails and three legged milking stools. How many cows did each girl have to milk, and did they do it early morning and late afternoon? At that time milk would have been supplied to all the local shops and houses from farms such as this. Today, milkmen like Tom Richardson get their milk from a sometimes quite distant, central source and deliver by milk float for miles around.

Taken from the highest point in Marple, All Saints church tower, this view shows how agricultural land has disappeared drastically over the last few decades. The original picture was taken when building work had commenced on the Manchester overspill site, adjacent to Hawk Green in the 1960s. Since then the erosion of farming land in the picture has continued, with every available piece of land being built upon including the expansion of industrial units behind the Goyt Mill, which of course no longer boasts its chimney. The older picture still shows plenty of open space despite the construction work, whilst the only green still visible today is the Marple golf course.

Bill Stiff ran his shop, situated next to the Texaco garage, for many years selling greengroceries, flowers and some general products. Local photographer David Brindley caught him sweeping up one day in 1998. Shops like Stiff's were once the source of everybody's domestic needs, today they have all but been replaced by large supermarkets such as the Co-op Superstore! As seen in the modern photograph, the shop has since been converted into flats and Bill is sadly with us no more.

There have been many changes around the Jolly Sailor Area. On the site of the garage stood the ancient Peace Farm demolished in the 1937. It was the original home of the Bradshaws and was the birthplace of John Bradshaw, 'regicide' - so called because his was the first signature on the execution warrant for Charles I!

91

In 1898 the Co-op opened their new building on Market Street opposite their grocery store. It housed a drapery and a butchers shop. The land and building cost £2,556 , 9s, 11d and it was said 'the building has an imposing appearance and is of a substantial character and its clock and tower constitute it a useful and ornamental feature of Marple.' That is still true today, although the building is no longer owned by the Co-op. The Co-op replaced the butchers shop with a shoe business. The modern photograph shows the present occupiers of the shops, the Helen Winterson dress shop and a telephone store.

Buses no longer run along Market Street so there is no longer a need for a bus stop. The photograph was taken just before the street was pedestrianised in the early 1970s. Plans for the complete redevelopment of the centre of Marple, that included multi-storey car park and supermarket, were abandoned when the developers went bankrupt. More modest improvements, including the exclusion of traffic from Market Street and Derby Way, were then carried out. The shops have changed hands a number of times in the last thirty years as can be seen in the modern photograph.

The shop, whose sign reads Clog and Boot Exchange, occupied a site now used as offices on Stockport Road. A shop where you could exchange your footwear! A sign that Marple was not all that prosperous in the early years of the last century when the photograph was taken when all the mill hands would have worn clogs. The shop seems to be closed with a blind over the window but the stands of shoes are still outside, maybe it was lunchtime. Edmund Croft, boot and shoe dealer traded there in 1907. The shop to the immediate right had its frontage altered in the 1920s so that it looked grand enough to become the District Bank but is now home to Ainsley Richard, Hairdresser.

The bay window and garden with railings have disappeared but otherwise the scene is recognisable. The three shops to the right of the picture are still in existence today although changing hands regularly, and sometimes remaining vacant for many months.

A photograph of M. Lomas & Son's, family butchers in the early 1900s. The shop, a big one with three large windows, was on the end of the block on Stockport Road and Elmley Street. It was the practice of local butchers to slaughter animals on their premises, so it was a common sight to see these animals being led into the back yards of butchers shops.

Today, the row has been replaced by a 1970s concrete block. Meat arrives at butchers these days in vans and is sold in many different ways from a hundred years ago. Chicken Tikka and Lamb Henry's were not the food of mill workers.

If you look at the cut-out hung up

over the door you can see that the shop next to the butchers must have sold shoes, more upmarket than the clogs and boots from the shop further up the road.

Worralls Ironmongers shop stood opposite the Navigation pub. You could have bought anything from wheelbarrows to carpet sweepers, from saucepans to wood supplies. A vast array of goods were displayed outside the shop and in the window, even petrol was sold!

Today 'Mulligans' on Stockport Road (pictured) and 'Hollins Building Supplies' on Hollins Lane offer most of the goods Worralls used to sell. 'The Hollins' sells many plants both annuals and perennials, but Shell petrol is now the preserve of petrol stations like Yeates on Stockport Road. Today, Worralls shop has been sub-divided and contains an Insurance agent/building society and an Indian takeaway!